AS SEEN IN THE ESPN 30 FOR 30 DOCUMENTARY "WHAT CARTER LOST" AND PORTRAYED IN THE FEATURE FILM "CARTER HIGH: A TRUE STORY"

FROM A LETTERMAN TO A BETTER MAN

A MEMOIR OF FIRST DOWNS AND SECOND CHANCES

PATRICK "PK" WILLIAMS
WITH ANGIE RANSOME-JONES

From A Letterman to a Better Man

Copyright © 2018 by Patrick "PK" Williams, with Angie Ransome-Jones (Samone Publishing)

All rights reserved. No part of this book may be reproduced or transmitted in any form or by any means without written permission from the author(s).

ISBN: 978-0-692-06809-0

Samoné Publishing
P.O. Box 163
Cedar Hill, Texas 75106-0163

www.samonepublishing.com

SENTIMENTS

"PK first came to me from South Grand Prairie High school. I remember him always being an interesting and unique kid and full of personality. I already had another Patrick Williams on the team, so I said – "I gotta' change one of y'alls names," and that's how he got his nickname. PK got out there and hustled and did what he was supposed to do and turned out to be a really good football player. He was a great addition to our team. All of my boys were just like sons to me. I was shocked to hear about the incidents that happened and especially that PK was involved because he was always such a good and respectful kid. I'll never forget, I was in my yard sweeping leaves when I got the call. I've always wished that I had known earlier because I may have been able to give them some type of counseling or even report them to their parents. But that wasn't in God's plan... Now I'm just so happy for him and that he turned to God. I've always considered him to be like one of my sons. I love him and I never stopped loving him just because he made a mistake; he turned his life around and that's all that matters. While he was incarcerated, I prayed for him and all of my boys so I'm happy I'm still around to see my prayers come to pass.

—**Coach Freddie James**
Former Head Football Coach,
David W. Carter High School

"I was happy to hear that Patrick Williams was writing a book and getting a chance to tell his story. My hope is that through the sharing of his experience, perhaps another young person will avoid the tumultuous path he had to travel down to realize his purpose. Although I was the counsel for one of the others that was accused at the time, I remember Patrick well and am not surprised he has come out on top again. I commend him for taking this huge leap of seeking forgiveness for his mistakes and hope that his story of redemption will help our community to continue in the healing process."

—Royce West
Texas State Senator, District 23
Managing Partner, West & Associates L.L.P.

"Patrick 'PK Williams has a story to tell, a story of redemption. As a TV journalist, I covered the trial of Patrick and the others from Carter High. But it wasn't until after he got out of prison that I came to know the man PK had become – a man of faith and family. A man I am proud to call a friend and a Brother in Christ."

—Richard Ray
TV Anchor/Reporter (KDFW/Fox 4)

"Well, as they say, you can't have a testimony without a test. I have personally witnessed my homie, Patrick "PK" Williams, not only be tested, but pass on so many levels. PK is the only person I KNOW to transfer to Carter and start; almost immediately, on the varsity football team. That alone was almost unheard of. And add the fact that he also became a captain on the team, was quite a feat! I was able to witness PK's heroics as a teenager at Carter and I've also seen him bounce back from trials and tribulations to become the outstanding man he is today. To witness PK's rise from the ashes and soar as an upstanding citizen is very inspiring. PK refused to stay down after a major setback. He refused to let that ten-count catch him. He got back up on his feet and took life by the horns and prevailed! We look for miracles all the time, and sometimes they're closer than you think, as PK has proven. Much success in the future, brother!"

—**Arthur Jordan Muhammad**
Director, Carter High: The Movie

"'From a Letterman to a Better Man' is a true story that proves it's not where you line up in the game, it's where you finish! It's a coming-of-age story that shows even though you make mistakes, you can make good, even when you come from the hood. I commend PK for sharing his deepest thoughts about the crimes that shook Dallas; but even more importantly, shook his world."

—**Ed Gray**
David W. Carter Alumnus and Dallas
TV political commentator (WFAA-TV)

"I had the privilege and blessing to meet and work with Patrick through my Court's Empowerment Program [supplemental felony probation program]. Patrick used his experiences to motivate and educate my felony probationers. I applaud him for sharing his powerful message with others through this book. Congratulations for turning your pain into purpose!"

—Amber Givens-Davis

Dedication

To my wife, I dedicate this book. Thank you for your patience, love, friendship and humor. I'm grateful for all the wonderful memories we have made together over the last 23 years. Even in the bad times, we made it through and never gave up on each other. You are my virtuous woman. You are a woman of strength and wisdom. I'm thankful to have you in my life.

I love you Latrina Williams

From The Heart of "PK"

I wrote this book, my memoir, as a way for my readers to experience my life's journey, which is still "a work in progress." When I look back on my life and everything I have experienced, I am most known for the Carter High School football "scandal," which I can truly say I am thankful for, because it helped to shape and mold me into the man I am today. But please know that this scenario *did not* and *will not* define me....*ever*.

I am always telling people that "I am more than what I come from," and what I mean by that is, that despite my rough start in life and what most would consider "humble beginnings," I am a KING in God's eyes and in the eyes of those who love me. I consider myself blessed and I am truly thankful for all I have experienced in my life – the good and the bad.

I hope that everyone who reads this book is truly blessed by it. It is written from my vantage point and in my own voice, which was very important for me because I want everyone who reads it to hear *me* throughout these precious pages – from the way that I talk to the way that I love.

When I am gone, what I want others to remember the most about me is that I was a family man, that I loved my wife, my kids and my grandkids; but that most of all, I loved God. He redeemed me and He saved me...

TABLE OF CONTENTS

Foreword ....,..*xiii*

Prologue..*xv*

Introduction 1

The Letterman 3

Three Years, Four Months and 19 Days 19

Cathy Hines 31

A Better Man 37

The Apology 49

Acknowledgments 57

Foreword

By Latrina "Trina" Williams

Who would have ever thought that we would be standing here 23 years later? I remember when we first met and feeling scared to ever love again. It was scary to even think about bringing another man around Terry and Marshel, but you showed me something that I never experienced: consistency. You started proving yourself, not only to me but to our children. Six months into our relationship, you let me know that you were committed for the long haul. Then you popped the question!

Not a day went by in which I felt like I needed more time to get to know you. Many questioned our relationship early on, but you remained steady. You stood beside me and we have proven them wrong. We have been through so many trials and disappointments throughout our marriage, and even questioned if we would make it through. You never left. When money was low, you were there. When the kids were acting crazy, you were there. When I lost my twenty something figure, I was always beautiful in your eyes. You always assured me that things would be alright and they were. You are a praying man and you have lifted our family through all the tough times. Only God knew you would be the best person to bring balance to my life.

What I love the most about our marriage is that we built it together. When you took a loss, I took a loss. When you gained, I gained. The losses were numerous, but your love never wavered. Do you remember the time when we were down to one car and the money was low? You looked at me and said, "If I have to ride this bike, I will so that you can use the car to take the kids to school." At that moment, I knew that God had sent me someone who was extra special. The respect that I have for you as my husband, my lover, and the father of my children has grown stronger day by day. When you encounter a setback, I have learned to sit back and watch my man come back stronger, because I trust you with my heart, my well-being and our family.

I love you Mr. Patrick Keith Williams, until death do us part. I am so proud of you for taking this huge leap of faith and revealing to the world what I already know about you.

Prologue

by Ed Gray

In the ESPN *30 for 30* documentary "What Carter Lost," it was said that if you lived in Dallas and you were Black, there were two types of people: Those who went to Carter High School and those who wished they did. Several decades later that is still true for many. Patrick Williams reached the zenith of fame early in his life, by being a football player on one of the greatest high school football teams in America.

He had it all, including the adulation of the community and a bright future ahead. For any youth, the pull of the streets can be intoxicating. School days are fleeting and with each decision made comes adult consequences. Patrick's decisions were more than just youthful indiscretions; those decisions have been the catalyst in his transition from boy to man.

This book captures why PK participated in the Carter High football robberies. It is also a confession of contrition. Incarceration is about paying penance. PK offers this book as a way of paying a lifetime penance for a short period of delinquency. From incarceration to redemption, PK Williams has come a long way. From our conversations, Patrick has displayed a humble spirit, but just as importantly he has borne the responsibility of his actions. These actions not only affected him, but impacted an entire community.

We are both members of that community, the Carter High School family. As it has been said many times, "All Hail Carter High." This book is not about praise. It is about achievement and overcoming obstacles.

Introduction

by Angie Ransome-Jones

Prior to my move to Texas from Mannheim, Germany in 1985, I knew relatively little about the Lone Star State except for the fact that I was born there on an army base, and that everything truly *is* bigger in Texas – from the hair, to the houses, to the football – especially the football.

I recall seeing the movie *Friday Night Lights* and the portrayal of the "other team," never realizing at the time that there was a story behind the story (there always is); the story of the greatest team that never was, as some would say. But as a believer in God, His grace and the supernatural power of redemption, this story's ending is quite the contrary for me now that I know the journey of Patrick "PK" Williams. From my first conversation with PK, I knew there was something special about this gentle giant – that "it" factor that not too many of us are gifted with in our lifetimes. Two hours after sitting down with him for the first time and hearing his personal testimony, I had no doubt that his story must be told. Not from the angle that has already been told so vividly on the "big screen" and the TV screen, but from the heart of one of the kindest and humblest men I've ever met in these 48 years of mine.

So as the story goes, there once was a high school football team named the Carter Cowboys from David W. Carter High School out of Oak Cliff, Texas. In 1988, they reigned as the greatest football team regionally and are still known today as one of the most talented in the history of Texas high school football. The Carter Cowboys were on their way to winning the state championship until an investigation involving the leading scorer's algebra grade deterred their dream; but only temporarily. After an ensuing legal battle, which nearly kept them out of the playoffs, the team was ruled ineligible but later eligible after a series of court battles in which the parents and the community, as a whole, stood behind the team. Long story short, they ended up winning the football championship, becoming the first Dallas team to win a championship since 1950.

Five days later, after winning state, three football players robbed a Jack in the Box, which would be the first of 21 robberies that police connected to 15 Carter neighborhood teenagers, six of whom played on the Carter Cowboys football team. All six were sent to prison with sentences ranging from two to 25 years. Finally, in 1991, Carter was stripped of its championship due to a loophole that made the arrests a violation of the No Pass/No Play rule in Texas. Since that time, Carter remains the last inner-city team to "win" a Texas state title in football.

In retrospect, although each member of the infamous "Carter Boys" had his day in court and the subsequent opportunity to offer a public apology to all those affected, PK's biggest regret, he says, is not being able to offer a personal apology in his own words, his own voice and to the larger community he feels he personally let down by what he refers to as his "bad decision." I am thankful to be able to help Patrick in offering that apology, in the form of this memoir. My prayer is that his readers will graciously accept it, embrace him and wholeheartedly support this great man of God, who is now a better man.

Chapter 1

The Letterman

And we know that in all things God works for the good of those who love him, who 'have been called according to his purpose.
~Romans 8:28~

My interest in football comes from my brother Michael, who was a beast in the game! My brother played for Lancaster High School as a fullback and defensive tackle. He was 6'2, about 230 pounds and was very, very good. He blocked for one of the best running backs in the state of Texas at the time, Roderick Gibbs. The year was 1985. My brother was a junior and I was a freshman. I had every intention of going to Justin F. Kimball High School to play football since my cousins stayed in Fawn Ridge Apartments, which is in the same district

PK Williams: Senior picture with State Football Medal.

as Kimball. Back in the 80's, that was the spot to be! My cousin's nickname was G-Rock and all the girls loved him. He was very popular at Kimball, which was another one of the reasons I wanted to be a Kimball Knight.

Some of the stupid stuff we would do is what we called "Negro knock," going door-to-door and kicking and knocking on it as hard as possible, and then we would take off running. Another thing we would do was "rock cars." Fawn Ridge was a built-in valley; one set of apartments on one side and a whole entire set on the other side. At night we would get rocks and horse apples and be on each side of the street and when a car would drive by; well, you know what happened next…

My brother had major knee surgery going into his senior year which pretty much kept him from playing. He ended up walking on at Navarro Junior College and played on the offensive line but then decided to come home after two years.

I went to several elementary schools and two different junior high schools. During my freshman year, we moved to Lancaster so that my brother could finish playing football there and that was really my first year playing. I was 5'9 and about 180 pounds my freshman year. They put me on defense as a defensive end.

We had two-a-days back then, which was really hard because we had to be at practice at 7:00 a.m. and would work out for about three hours and be back at 3:00 p.m. to practice for another three hours. Man, I hated two-a-days because the coaches would run us into the ground! We did everything from running drills to bear crawls but that was supposed to make you good. Lancaster High School

The Letterman

The Ladder of Success.

in the mid-to-late 80's was pretty much 95% white, and so was Desoto and Cedar Hill. Desoto, at that time, was Lancaster's rival. I had a pretty good freshman year considering it was my first time ever playing football. I made a lot of quarterback sacks and scored a touchdown off of a fumble recovery. But I also ended up failing the first six weeks of classes and because of No Pass No Play, I missed about four games of a ten-game season.

In Texas, the summers are very hot and dry, but it's also the time to work out and get ready for the upcoming football season. I remember going into my sophomore year with some goals in mind; my number one goal was not to fail. Our football team that year went 10 and 0. I had another great football season.

During my freshman and sophomore years at Lancaster, I can say I was a pretty good kid. In fact, I think my only "bad decision" was made during the time I had unprotected sex with this pretty young bright-skinned girl, who blessed me with my son, Keith. I consider him to be one of the biggest blessings of my life.

Around the time of my first-time fatherhood experience, my mama had found a townhome in south Grand Prairie that was cheaper than where we were staying, so we packed up and moved. I really didn't know what to expect when I first got to South Grand Prairie High School (SGP), but I remember just being amazed because it looked like a college. It had the best facilities that I had ever laid eyes on. The varsity locker room was huge with oversized lockers, good football equipment and a great weight room. When I was introduced to the coaching staff they seemed really excited to have me. I was excited too because Coach Edwin Patton, who has since gone home to be with the Lord, was a great coach and it gave me the opportunity to play with an all-state linebacker named Reggie Barnes, who later went on to play professional ball.

Me and Reggie had really good chemistry on the field, so the coaches decided on moving me from defensive end to defensive tackle, which I excelled at. Looking back, I believe that it was at SGP that my true potential was uncovered. The whole atmosphere at SGP was great, but my home life was quite the opposite. My mama was struggling to pay bills so we had to move out of one townhouse into another that was cheaper and smaller. At times, we didn't have anything to eat. My Auntie Linda; who was a close family friend stayed one townhouse down from ours and she helped feed us. When our lights would get turned off, we would run an extension cord down to her house so we could plug up a lamp to do our homework.

When we ended up getting evicted, I had to stay with the next-door neighbor for the rest of the school year so I wouldn't miss playing for the season. I took an extra job at Jack in the Box, which is where I learned how to make a double-double cheeseburger. But then my Mama decided that it was a better move for me to stay at my aunt's house in Oak Cliff, which is how I ended up at David W. Carter High School.

Mama was locked up at the time due to writing some hot checks, so my brother had to come home and unenroll me from SGP, which was extremely hard for me. I'll never forget -- all the coaches stood in line and gave me hugs. Man, they really hated to see me go and I hated it too. To this very day, I have so much respect for the SGP coaches; especially Coach Patton. Apparently, they really cut for me, too. I found out later that one of my teachers, Ms. Ann Pogue, had contemplated adopting me so that I could stay at SGP.

I didn't understand it at first because I really clowned in this lady's class, but she never once sent me to the principal's office. In fact, she ended up being a character witness in my trial. My attorney called her and was blown away because she spoke nothing but good things about me. Imagine, a young white woman speaking on the behalf of a young Black man. After reconnecting with her years later she said she felt like I would get into trouble at Carter. She didn't want to see that happen because of all the potential she saw in me. That, to me, spoke volumes about not only her, but the potential that others saw in me and that God saw in me, too. And even though Ms. Pogue considered taking me in, she admitted that after sitting down with her husband and all things considered, they decided it wasn't the best decision for her family, which is why I never knew.

When I got to Carter, I didn't know much about it except for the countless stories my cousin had told me. I expected the cute females, the wild parties and the shenanigans. What I *did* know about the Carter Cowboys was that a *cat* named Jessie Armstead, who was a three-time All-American, played there. In my mind, I just knew this cat couldn't have been better than Reggie Barnes; but as it turned out, he really was. He was faster and colder.

It was the Spring of 1988 when I arrived at Carter to finish out my junior year. It was a life-changing experience because it was "all the way live" at Carter. At the time, I was about 5'10" and weighed in around 195 pounds and I was very handsome, of course. I signed up for football and remember meeting the legendary Coach Freddie James standing in the lunchroom. I boldly walked right up to him and introduced myself and told him what position I played. I remember him giving me this look and saying, "You a little small to be playing defensive tackle." All I could say in response was, "Just give me a chance Coach."

Never in my whole entire life had I seen so many pretty girls just everywhere you looked at Carter; I mean they were fine as wine and all shades of black, light brown, dark brown and *jet black*. Wow, I loved them all! It took me less than a week to realize I was back in the hood. To go from two all-white, suburban schools to an all-Black school like Carter was a culture shock for me, but it was also good to be amongst my people again. And while I do regret the robberies that landed me in jail, I don't regret my Carter experience as a whole. I wouldn't trade it for the world because of the love we all had for each other there.

When I first got to Carter, I knew I had to make a name for myself and in order to do that I would have to be really good in football. I mean, some of these cats had been playing football since little league all the way up to high school. You had legends like Darren Lewis who was the greatest running back to come out of Carter. Then you had players like Jimmie Hall, Clifton Abraham, Jessie Armstead, Joe Burch, Leshai Maston, Derrick Evans and Chris Calhoun. I mean there are so many great players, so I knew I was going to love me some Carter High!

Because I had been working at the Jack in the Box in Grand Prairie, I was able to transfer to the location on Polk closer to home. But I was so focused on starting for the best high school football team in Texas and nothing else mattered. Although the facilities and the equipment were very different (and I mean, *a lot* different), than what I was used to at SGP, the thing I liked the best was Coach James' office. It was filled with pictures of every college player that had ever played for him; some of the most gifted players in the country. I'll never forget the time I was in his office when the San Francisco 49'ers called to inquire about one of his players at the time, Chet Brooks, who played cornerback for us. They asked about his character, his skills, ability; and of course Coach had nothing but good things to say. That, to me, not only spoke to the caliber of our team, but just how much Coach James believed in all of us; as well as how much he was admired and respected on and off the field. It didn't take long for me to make a name for myself either on the team. The funny thing was, there was another cat there named Patrick Williams, who later went on to coach the Carter Cowboys. To keep from getting us mixed up, Coach James called me "PK," which is how I got my nickname. I had a great Spring practice. So much so, that they gave me a starting spot. But that came with some drama because the UIL (University Interscholastic League) thought I had been recruited from SGP. Me and my auntie had to go downtown to meet with the Superintendent and the principal from SGP had to come and testify too. In the end, because our stories added up, the case ended up being closed.

After a great spring workout they gave me a starting spot. As a starter at Carter, I became very popular very fast. The first friend I made was a gifted left-handed running back named Carlos Allen. We called him "Los," and we would hang out every day. We still keep in touch until this very day. Me and Los had birthdays around the same time.

I'll never forget the time we rented out a hotel room on Camp Wisdom. And although it was a last-minute thing, everybody got word and showed up and showed out! I mean, we kicked it hard! Me and Los had a true brotherly love and he actually introduced me to the rest of our crew, which we called the "9 8 Posse." Keith Campbell was another one I also considered to be "my boy." He was extremely smart and a natural-born leader.

I remember one Saturday night we went across the bridge because, at the time, Oak Cliff was "dry." In order for us to get something to drink we'd have to drive to south Dallas, which was across the bridge. All the other fellas were getting 40-ounces of malt liquor and other hard liquor.

The Letterman

I walked up and put my apple juice on the counter. I remember Keith looking at me and saying, "Negro what you drinking?"

When I told him I didn't drink, he laughed and said, "Well Negro you gonna drink tonight!"

It was that night I got introduced to Boones Farm and beer. Before I got to Carter, I had never drunk or smoked anything, but folks swore I was always high because I was always so hyped up! So now when people ask me if I thought the fellas I hung out with were a bad influence on me, since I never got into any serious trouble until my Carter days, I always say no and I mean that. These guys truly came from "good stock," grew up in the best neighborhoods; the opposite of where I grew up, but they never treated me any differently. We all had real love for each other. Plus, when it boils down to it, I made my own decisions and, if anything, being around those guys just made me better and work harder because of how talented those cats were and how much harder they worked to get to that level.

So, while I wasn't as close as the other guys that I got into trouble with, we all still had love for each other. Norbert Rodgers didn't play for Carter. He was Derrick's cousin, which meant we were tight by default. Jimmy Edwards didn't play football either, but we became close because we ended up doing our time on the same penitentiary unit and looked after each other while we were locked up. Gary Edwards was the cat that was part of the original grading controversy drama. He and Derrick ended up doing separate robberies outside of what me and Keith and Los did.

Leading up to the end of our season, we had to beat Odessa Permian in order to get to the state championship title. They were the team in the *Friday Night Lights* movie.

Even though all the games leading up to it were all hard fought, I remember the championship game the most because I got the opportunity to play at Texas Stadium and all of our names were written above the lockers. Nothing could compare to seeing my name up there! It was like a dream because we could not believe that after all the mess we had been through, all of the court dates, the appeals, getting on and off the bus and all of the ups and downs, that we made it to the state championship game. And everybody knows that it gets no bigger than playing in the state championship game in Texas, and we were the first DISD (Dallas Independent School District) school to play in a state championship game since 1960. There was even a song that came out around the time by Nemesis called "Only in Oak Cliff" and one of the lyrics in it said, "You much harder because you're from David W. Carter." There was so much excitement because we were playing for the entire community.

We were playing for Kimball, South Oak Cliff, Roosevelt, our moms, our dads, uncles and grandparents! This was a very special and proud moment for the City of Dallas and we did not disappoint. Our offense and defense dominated the entire game, and with that we won. The celebration that followed was nothing short of amazing. Holding the state championship trophy after the game was indescribable. I still get goosebumps just thinking about it.

So after our big win and the season was over, we were on cloud nine and our popularity at school and in the community was at an all-time high. We were like movie stars, rock stars, and celebrities and with that status, we could have any girl we wanted and pretty much *anything* we wanted. We spent a lot of time rolling around in my auntie's car; "the bucket," we called it, bumpin' NWA and drinking 40 ounces like they were water. Redbird Mall and Kiest Bazaar were our regular hangouts where we would admire all the gold chains and other stuff we *didn't* need.

It was around that same time that I started observing the operations at the Jack in the Box. I made mental notes of where the cameras were and especially the Friday night operation when all the money got counted. I mentioned the idea to my cousin first, and then to Los about how we could "come up." He then took the plan to Keith and together we said, "Let's do it!"

My auntie had a .22 pistol with a pearl handle that I got out of her dresser drawer, Los had a .32 and Keith had a .45. We thought that was all we needed. Thinking about it now, I admit that we weren't just caught up, but we were real immature and just plain dumb. We had everything going for us, but still we wanted more.

On the night of the first robbery, I can remember how nervous I was; to the point where it felt like I could hear my own heartbeat. I had gone out to move the camera so my manager, the cook and the other cat that was working that night wouldn't see Keith and Los coming in. So, when I first saw them with those stocking caps on, I started laughing and I kept laughing even when they told us to get down on the floor, which made the cook suspicious of me. I remember he just kept saying to me, "Man, you in on this," which may have ended up causing us to get busted in the end.

The police didn't question me until later, but I remember my heart racing and looking at the clock just anxious to get off work. I had my cousin come and pick me up that night then we met up with Keith and Los to count all of the money. When I got back to the house, my auntie was in her room asleep so my cousin Marci had to let me in through the window. I threw the bag of money on the bed and before the bills could even hit the sheets, she started grabbing it and putting it her pockets and anywhere else she could stash it. It was the funniest thing to see how excited she was. It turned out to be about five or six thousand dollars. We ended up giving our homeboy Sean some cash, even though he decided at the last minute not to do the robbery with us. We respected him just that much and even more so later when we realized that he made the *right* decision.

When the police did end up questioning me; instead of them asking me about the details of what happened the night before, they were more interested in me as a Carter Cowboy than as a person of interest. We even ended up chopping it up about what a great season we had, which made me feel even more untouchable. Plus, I remember every time we got ready to rob, we always jammed out to either NWA, Too Short or some type of gangsta' rap that would get us all hyped up to the point where we could visualize ourselves like the characters in the song, doing everything they rapped about. The music was like a drug to us at the time, the two went hand in hand.

Being the *dummies* that we were back then, we went straight to Redbird Mall that night and I remember the first thing I bought was a Turkish rope chain. Our shopping spree continued Saturday and Sunday and by that Monday morning when we hit the Carter halls, we were "gold down to the ground." The word on the street was that we were selling dope, but nobody dared to question us because of our "celebrity" status. So not long after that, I ended up quitting Jack in the Box. Me, Keith and Los got a job at Panchos restaurant. It didn't take us long to scope it out, learn the operation and realize this spot was going to be an *even bigger* jackpot than Jack in the Box. We set our plan in action to rob Panchos twice. For the first run, we ended up adding Jimmy and Norbert into the mix. Again, we always hit on a Friday night since that was the busiest night. We knew none of us who worked there could go in because somebody would recognize our voices. I'll never forget when Jimmy was trying to unload the gun and it went off accidentally. That was one of the scariest moments of my life. It was like everything went in slow motion. When I think about it now and how

PK Williams (Number 79) on all out blitz.

reckless and selfish and stupid we were, and the fact that somebody could've gotten seriously hurt, I just thank God for His mercy and grace and for sparing our lives and the other innocent lives that could've been taken. That time around, we got away with even more cash; close to seven or eight grand, but that still wasn't enough. But after the second Panchos robbery, me and Los decided to turn in our robbing card. It was just too much of a risk. Plus, during that time, there was so much going on with graduation and recruiters calling and getting letters from some of the smaller schools. I was so confused at the time and really wasn't sure what I was going to do. I just wasn't interested in going to college, partly because I knew realistically that I wouldn't be able to start and partly because I just didn't think college was for me. Graduating was exciting because it marked a milestone in my life. With over 200 unexcused absences and a few failed classes, I knew it was nothing but God's grace, coupled with my favored football status that allowed me to graduate on time.

Fast forward to not too long after graduation, we found out on the news that Derrick had been caught. News spread like wildfire and, at first, we weren't worried because he didn't rob with us. But about a week after that crew got caught, there was speculation about a robbing spree and that others could be involved. That's when we started getting worried.

The day they came to pick me up and took me down to the police station, I was staying with my auntie. I had no doubt what it was all about when I saw the officers at the door. Our only regret at the time was us not telling our families first. When we talked about it later, we all agreed that we should've gone to our parents but we were scared to tell. We didn't want them to be disappointed in us, in the case that we *didn't* end up getting caught. It sounds crazy now, but that was just our mindset at the time. And although we don't think that the blow would've been lessened, maybe our families could've "lawyered up" or been better prepared for what was to come, at least.

Chapter 2

Three Years, Four Months and 19 Days

Be sure of this: The wicked will not go unpunished, but those who are righteous will go free.
~Proverbs 11:21~

We were sentenced on a Friday, and believe it or not, that week leading up to our sentencing was the most at peace I had ever felt. Mama had just started attending Lighthouse Church in Dallas and shortly after my arraignment, I started going too. The mothers of the church were just so loving and supportive. They kept telling me, "everything is gonna be okay" and I truly believed that. God just kept nudging me to draw closer to him. So I did. I started reading my Bible and started craving the Word, and God just became so *real* in my life. For the first time ever, I felt something greater than me.

It was a Tuesday in September, just days away from us going before the judge. I'll never forget being in my room when the Holy Spirit walked in and filled me with God's spirit. I started speaking in tongues and everything! At the time I was so filled with sin that, in that moment, it felt like a burden had been lifted off my

From A Letterman to A Better Man

Our sentencing day in court.

shoulders. I remember calling Mother Austin at the church because I was so moved. Then I spent that last Tuesday, Wednesday and Thursday in my room, just reading my Bible and crying. But the tears were tears of joy and relief because I felt the indescribable love of God.

On the day of the sentencing, the whole courthouse was packed, like it was a celebrity trial. My classmates cut school to come to the courthouse and I had a few girlfriends at the time that came too. Everybody wanted to see what they could see, but only immediate family was allowed in the courtroom.

I had on a gray suit, my wingtip shoes and was cloaked in God's favor. Plus, I had a pretty good lawyer, so I wasn't really worried about anything. In fact, I was very calm. My family had pooled their money together, but even with that, my grandmamma had to put up her ring so that I could make bail and afford an attorney. I

Three Years, Four Months And 19 Days

felt bad about that, but my Uncle Ce had made up his mind that we were going to get us the best that *our* money could buy to make sure we beat this thing. George White was very good and thorough. He even reserved a court house where we could role play and do a mock trial to make sure I was prepared. I remember him telling me to just tell the truth about everything because if I told a lie, I would have to remember that lie. So, I did just that – I told the truth. When the judge asked, I told him I did it because I wanted gold chains, and that was the truth. The judge called us one by one and we stood up. As he read our sentences off, everyone was in disbelief and stunned, and some were even crying. It was total chaos because no one expected us to get sentenced. I remember Judge Joe Kendall saying that we had done more robberies than Bonnie and Clyde, and the only difference was that they were murderers and we didn't kill anyone. To me, it was a drastic and unfair comparison.

People didn't understand why I was smiling and laughing when they led us away, but it was because I was filled with the Holy Spirit and the mothers of the church had all been praying for me. It really didn't matter what happened to me. In my mind, I was thinking, *"Man,* I'm about to be locked up." But because I had Him, I was free! I didn't care what happened because I knew He was with me. I had the peace of God all over me; a peace that surpassed all understanding. I knew God was with me and would protect me like he had done before and not just with the suicide attempt, but also from an incident that took place before we were arrested.

A guy I had been "beefing with" pulled out a gun on me the spring before. I'll never forget it. I was in the Tom Thumb parking lot off Camp Wisdom and Polk in Dallas. I was literally staring down the barrel of a gun and I guess with people looking and the threat of being caught, he decided not to shoot. It just wasn't my time and I knew then, too, that God was with me. When He is with you, it doesn't matter what you're going through. You can endure anything!

The judge ended up sentencing me to 13 years, but my "time served" ended up being three years, four months and nineteen days. From the courtroom, they escorted us to the holding cell and we didn't talk much. We were still in shock from our sentences. From there, they put us on "the chain," and took us down to Lew Sterrett County Jail where we got processed. That's one of the pictures everybody is used to seeing.

While we were waiting we watched the news and it was just so surreal looking at ourselves and seeing everybody's reaction. It wasn't really until then that I realized the magnitude of what I had done and that what we did affected not just our families, but the whole community.

We got out of Lew Sterrett in about two weeks then they put us on the chain again and hauled us off to the Texas Department of Corrections (TDC) and then on to Huntsville to get processed.

When we first got to the penitentiary, they weighed us and counted our tattoos. We were in a holding room for a couple of hours before they took us to our cells, not knowing what we were going to be faced with next.

Was I scared? *Oh yeah*! You hear all these stories about Big Bubba trying to get ya' booty, but luckily all of us could fight. Prison was real serious, but we were like "movie stars" in there. We were famous criminals and, as crazy as it sounds, we craved that attention because we were young and immature.

After all of us were processed, we ended up in different units. I ended up in one in Navasota (TX) for a couple of months, which was close to Houston. They usually try to put you close to where you were raised, but not in my case. I eventually went to the field where I picked crops like watermelon, okra and beans. The field was where I also learned how to clean a fence line, like modern-day slavery...free labor. Although I hated it at the time, that skillset later turned out to be a blessing for me. A typical day usually started at 3 or 4 am. We got served breakfast, which was usually cereal or oatmeal. Sometimes we had pancakes. And, by the way, if you've ever seen anybody put peanut butter on their pancakes, just know they've been to prison. Just picture the pancakes being warm and the peanut butter melting on the pancakes like butter – it was one of the best meals I ever had while I was there. Lunch was usually around noon. They often served us goulash where they threw in everything they could find from noodles to cornbread and meats of all kinds. Dinner was around 5 pm and then we had recreation time starting at 7 pm when we played dominoes and cards or basketball, if we went outside. Then we shut it down usually around 9 or 9:30 pm. And each day was the same thing all over again.

In prison they provide you with the very basic necessities like a toothbrush, but with tooth powder instead of toothpaste. We also used homemade soap. You could take a shower as many times as you wanted but the bathroom was an open bathroom, so you know how that goes – it was best to handle your business and get out of there. Just as statistics show, the majority of the population in prison was Black or Hispanic, and yet and still racism still exists because the white boys got the better jobs; just like in the *free world*. I did some research on the statistics because I wanted to understand the numbers and here's what I found on the NAACP website:

- In 2014, African Americans constituted 2.3 million, or 34%, of the total 6.8 million correctional population.

- African Americans are incarcerated at more than 5 times the rate of whites.

- The imprisonment rate for African American women is twice that of white women.

- Nationwide, African American children represent 32% of children who are arrested, 42% of children who are detained, and 52% of children whose cases are judicially waived to criminal court.

- Though African Americans and Hispanics make up approximately 32% of the US population, they comprised 56% of all incarcerated people in 2015.

- If African Americans and Hispanics were incarcerated at the same rates as whites, prison and jail populations would decline by almost 40%.

Also in prison, you had certain classifications – if you were a low-risk classification, you could work on the outside of the gates or outside of the prison but that was much harder work. At the same time, you weren't watched over as much as you were inside of the prison. I landed a job in the stainless steel factory. I made those stainless steel commodes that you see in prison. I was the polisher, and a damn good one too. I intended on "laying it down" anyway so I did what I had to do. Layin' it down is when you don't feel like going to work, so you basically say, "I ain't goin," and they end up shipping you to another unit depending on how often you do it. I only did it so that I could get shipped back closer to the home. During recreation in the evening times, the Blacks and Hispanics used to fight. You had to do what you had to do. You never knew what was going to happen as a result of these fights.

While I still maintained my faith, I'll be honest – I really didn't spend much time in the Word or in prayer because of the lack of privacy and just because my focus had shifted to trying to stay alive, out of trouble and getting out of there. I know it was nothing but God's grace that got me through along with the regular visits from my mama. She brought my son with her when she came along with my brother and cousin Marci. She kept money on my books too. But I remember the reaction I had when she told me she sold my gold chains that I loved so much, in order to keep that money on my books. I can laugh about it now, but at the time it wasn't funny because those gold chains and jewelry, in general, was like a god to me. The weekly letters from Mama helped too, and served as a source of encouragement. They served as a constant reminder of who I belonged to and that I was loved.

After I "laid it down," they shipped me off to Palestine. They put me back in the fields, but because I had a blood cousin there who had some pull, he was able to get me a good job washing windows. I was just happy being there because that meant my plan of laying it down actually worked. I was closer to home and around people I was familiar with.

I was a pretty big dude back then so I never backed down from a fight, but as time went on, I didn't have as many fights because I was trying to do what I needed to do to get out. I wanted to make sure I was in good standing the closer I got to parole. Prisoners knew who we, *the Carter Boys*, were; so they didn't mess around with us as much as they could have. I had a couple of fights but didn't really have to form alliances because of who I was.

I remember working in a field and the bosses were the prison guards who rode horses. There was one they called Skeletor, an old white man on a horse who was just mean for no reason. They even had a sharp shooter that would shoot you if you took off running. Thank God I never saw anybody get shot. The closest I got to seeing death was when a dude killed another inmate with a shank he made out of a toothbrush. They locked us down for a couple of days but for us that meant no work, which was good. It also meant you get a sandwich, milk, juice and an orange, which wasn't so good. It seemed like we went on lockdown for a couple of times each month.

Imagine being around cats who had life sentences. Some of them never saw the light of day. To me, a lot of them got senseless sentences too; judges just throwing the book at these young men for no good reason. These youngsters get locked up and then by the time they realize that their way ain't' the right way, it's too late. While I was in, I met cats that had been in jail since they were 16-years old and many who were 30-years-old now but still had ten years or more left to serve because of petty crimes; whether it be selling drugs or unarmed robbery. Even our former President, Barack Obama has pointed out the disparities of our criminal justice system, time and time again. In his speech at the 106th NAACP National Convention, he had this to say about it:

Three Years, Four Months And 19 Days

"The bottom line is that in too many places, black boys and black men, Latino boys and Latino men experience being treated differently under the law....This is not just barbershop talk. A growing body of research shows that people of color are more likely to be stopped, frisked, questioned, charged, detained. African Americans are more likely to be arrested. They are more likely to be sentenced to more time for the same crime. And one of the consequences of this is, around one million fathers are behind bars. Around one in nine African American kids has a parent in prison."

While I was in prison I witnessed, firsthand, a judicial system that is not only prejudiced against black people, but one that has also sentenced innocent young black men to time in jail for crimes they did not commit. Luckily for me, I found a system that I am now proud to say I am caught up in and that I love and want to be in for the rest of my life – that system is called the Kingdom of God!

The chain gang.

All things considered, I can truly say that the justice system didn't help me because I had made up in my mind from Day 1 that once I got out, I wasn't going back. And as crazy as it sounds, you had cats that got out and then six months after, they were back in because they thought they could beat the system by selling dope instead of getting a job and trying to do things the right way.

My mind was made up. This was *not* how I wanted to live my life. I had a cell mate, an older dude, who always tried to tell me about life and his life experiences. At 45-years-old, he had been in jail six times…yes, six times!!! So to me, he was a six-time loser. I was thinking, *Fool, you 40 years old! It took you all that time to realize that you can't beat the system? You got kids that you barely know and a family that don't know you.* He couldn't tell me nothin' because of his own track record.

I told him, "Man, go kick rocks!" But I also understand that when you get caught up in the system, it's hard to get out. It's a whole different mindset and a different lifestyle. These youngsters get locked up and then by the time they realize that their way ain't the right way, it's too late.

Because I had laid it down, I had a low classification, which meant I was low-risk. This allowed me to bypass a standard parole hearing. So about a year-and-a-half or so before my release they sent me to Bridgeport, which was the pre-release station. It was there that I reunited with Los, Gary, Jimmy and Norbert and it was just like old times until my cancer scare.

Out of nowhere a big growth sprung out of my neck. They discovered it was a lymph node and the prison doctors convinced me that I had cancer and was going to die! That's when my faith kicked in again. I know it was nothing but the prayers of those who loved me that truly saved my life. They ended up sending me to a hospital in Galveston where they did surgery to remove the lymph node and let me recover. The node turned out to be non-cancerous, praise God! From there I ended up back in Palestine to finish my time.

When it was all said and done, I spent four Thanksgivings and four Christmases in prison. My grandmamma died in 1991 and they wouldn't even let me furlough to go to her funeral. The system didn't rehabilitate me at all. In fact, it made me angry and bitter in terms of how I was treated, like a slave – being told what to do, when to eat, when to go to work, when to go to sleep – and all for making a bad decision at a very young age. Where's the rehabilitation in that? I got released on a Friday, February 12, 1993. It was a gorgeous day and one of the most memorable days of my life. I had survived. I was free from prison and I was still young, and alive!

Chapter 3

Cathy Hines

A kindhearted woman gains honor,
but ruthless men gain only wealth
~Proverbs 11:16~

When I think about the events leading up to my "bad decision," I can hear my mama's voice so clearly, almost as if she's standing here today saying "Baby, if you keep on doing what you doing, you're not gonna make it...it ain't gonna end well." When I think about it now, even though she didn't know what we were actually doing in terms of the robberies, it was a warning sign from God because my mama was always very prophetic.

Cathy Hines, PK's mother.

My mama was like one of those moms you read about in a storybook. She loved her boys and *I* was her baby. She raised both me and my younger brother, Michael, and even though we had different dads, we were very close and always treated the same. Our family was small but always very close-knit. My grandmamma helped raise me too. She passed away when I was in prison and to this day I think about the fact that I couldn't go to her funeral, all because of my bad decision.

On Valentine's Day, we were those boys who got cards, candy and balloons. Mama came to *everything* we had at school. To me, that makes a big difference in a child's life to see their parent's face in the audience. Mama was a great cook too. She made sure we had home-cooked meals during the week. I remember her cooking liver and onions, tuna fish casserole, and baked fish. I also remember the days she would take us to work with her at Texas Power and Light where she had her own little office and couch. I really loved it when she took us to lunch at Thanksgiving Square. We were always real excited to go to work with her; especially on payday Fridays when we got treated to fried fish, which is still one of my favorites until this very day.

Mama did what she could to keep a roof over our heads, but we moved around so much, just so Mama could make ends meet. When rent went up, we moved. We became professional movers. I mean, we got really good at packing up stuff. One positive thing I can say that came out of it though, is that we made a lot of friends. It did get tough at times though. I'll never forget the day we got evicted from our house. That was a turning point for me and the first time I ever thought about taking my own life. It was just me and my mama because, by that time, my big brother was already in college. I came home from school and our furniture, clothes and everything was outside. I didn't know what to do. I wish I could remember his name, and maybe I don't because I blocked most of it out, but the guy next door came by and told me that my mama had called and told him that I needed to stay with him until we could get things all figured out. Mama was in jail at that time for writing bad checks. Again, she did what she could and the best she could to keep us fed and to keep a roof over our heads. I didn't know what I was going to do or what was to happen to me. As I walked around the complex, crying and grabbing my head, my mind was all over the place and I just thought it would be so much easier to end it all. There was this one street that had a lot of traffic and in that moment, I thought about just walking out into it. It would be quick and easy and hopefully painless. But God – I ended up walking back to the guy's house and stayed with him for about three weeks until it was time for Christmas break.

I think being evicted and convicted was a turning point for my mama too. She really became rooted in her faith when she got out after a couple of months. Mama had always attended church and even sent us to church when *she* didn't go. And whatever board she served on or committee or whatever it was, you best believe she was the president of it! Before she passed, she left her church home of years to join my church, which meant a lot to me.

In her later years, she also had a postcard ministry at church where she sent postcards to men and their families who were incarcerated. I truly believe that God gave her that ministry because of my situation. She wanted to get the message across to the young men and even to the older men to never lose hope and to always have faith in God. I remember getting letters like that from Mama when I was in the pen. Sometimes I got two to three letters a week from her; that's just the type of mother she was.

The love of my life, Cathy Hines, my Mama; ended up passing away from congenital heart failure in 2010 at age 59. One of the things I'm most grateful for is the fact that before she passed, she got to hear me preach the Word.

I often think about what my life would've been like if my Dad was in it, right there by her side raising us like the Cosby's. But I know that wasn't part of God's plan. I wish I could say I had some memory of him being around, but I don't. As young men, we crave our fathers because to have a father in your life is very important. He represents the structure of the household because that's how God designed it. It should be God first, your family second, the church, then the rest.

But I don't know my father, never even met him. I can remember going to my grandmamma's house, on my Dad's side, in the projects. I would go just to see if he would show up. He never did. Do I think it would've made a difference to have him in my life? Absolutely, because a father is supposed to help direct the child; especially a young man. Believe it or not, I don't harbor bitterness because I'm not a bitter person. I don't hold anger because I truly believe that *it's gonna' be what it's gonna'* be.

The place I'm in right now, I'm content, and I'm happy and have no complaints. Besides, I truly believe that me not having a father in my life has made me a better father to my own kids. The funny thing is, I did some so-called research and was able to track my father down a few years ago. I found out he stayed close by, in Arlington (TX), right down the road. So, after I tracked him down I called him, and this is what he told me: "Man, I'm sorry I wasn't there, your Mama wouldn't let me come around…"

I knew that wasn't the truth. But it didn't matter to me at the time because I just wanted to meet him. It was in the month of December when I made the call. I remember him saying, "Man, I got some time off in February we can meet."

And I just left it there.... I mean, it was December, and he lived less than 30 minutes away but was willing to wait another three months to meet me, his own son. If I were in his shoes, I would've broken my neck to meet my son right then and there, no questions asked. And that was the last time I ever spoke to him or spoke about him, until now...

Chapter 4

A Better Man

*The end of a matter is better than its beginning,
and patience is better than pride.*
~Ecclesiastes 7:8~

Being locked up for that length of time gave me a lot of time to think about my future plans, things I wanted to do and things I wanted to make right. When I was released, I was still young – 21 going on 22, to be exact. Trying to go to college wasn't something I wanted to do. Getting a job was at the forefront of my mind along with just getting myself together, spending lost time with my family, reconnecting with my son and getting back into church.

Even though I got out on a Friday, I didn't make it home to my family until that Monday because they only released you in the mornings and by the time I got to Huntsville from Palestine, it was almost nighttime. So, I took a bus from Huntsville to Dallas and by the time I made it home, Mama had gotten most of the family together and we went to Good Lucks where I had a link basket with extra toast. Needless to say, because I had spent so much time alone in jail, I had a lot of sexual

PK Williams, a better man.

tension built up, so getting with a female was also one of the first things I wanted to do. But because I was so used to picking and choosing who I wanted, I turned down the first couple of offers. But by the time I did get some, all I can say is that it was very, very powerful!

 Now that I was out, I stayed with my mama, of course. She had just retired with a good service package, and lived in a house in Oak Cliff. I didn't have a dime to my name – no car, no more jewelry, nothing. I had to start from scratch. Not a whole lot had changed since I went to prison, but a lot of my friends had gone off to college. I knew after we went in, it had gotten bad around the neighborhood in terms of crime. From what I had heard, the robbery rate went up, one of my classmates had gotten killed and things had just gotten bad in general. I started looking for work, and my Mama started trippin', telling me what time I needed to be home and writing out these long lists of things tellin' me what I needed to be doing. This wasn't working for me, so I called my brother. He let me move in with him in a real nice condo near downtown. He gave me two things to do, save money and get a car. Once I did that, we planned to move to Lancaster to a bigger place. During that time also, I reported to what seemed like a different parole officer every month, which continued until about 2003. I did everything I was supposed to do but, most importantly, I got a job. After a while, they trusted me and didn't require me to report on a regular basis.

I ended up getting on at a temporary agency called Manpower where Kellie, who was like a sister to me, worked and got me hired. My first assignment was in the bakery division at Sweetheart. I knew it was nothing but the grace of God that got me that job because nowhere on the application did it ask if I had ever been convicted of a felony; and we all know that's one of the first things they usually ask. Although I was assigned to the bakery division, they had me working outside and it was hot as hell outside, so I wasn't happy. I kept telling God, *"Now God, I just got outta prison doing this, mannnnn, I don't wanna' do this..."* But when it was all said and done, I cleaned that fence line so good and they were so impressed that they kept me around and hired me on permanently. This was confirmation for me of God working in my life. The very thing that I despised, God turned it around for my favor. With the money I made from working I was able to get me a 1987 Plymouth Reliant. Me and my brother moved into a two-bedroom in Lancaster.

When I wasn't working, I was usually in church from sun-up to sundown. When I got out I was just so grateful to be out and longed for the Word of God to be implanted back inside of me. After a while, I was ready to sew my wild oats, so I started hanging out with my boys Norbert and Los again. We hung out everywhere from the strip clubs to the pool halls and it was almost like reliving our earlier years. People thought we were professional football players and I guess we could've been. Even though technically we weren't supposed to be around each other while on parole, we were brothers and had a common bond that made it hard for us to separate.

The night I met my wife, we were up to our usual shenanigans. It was Mother's Day weekend. We went to a club called Beamers that was real hot at the time. Back then I was fit, not flabby like I am now. I had the confidence of a king and could pretty much still pull any girl I wanted. My wife was with her friend Jackie.

I'll never forget it – we were walking to our cars and I saw her from a distance. She was a fine, *pretty little black thang* so I hollered out across the parking lot, "Heyyyyy, you right there!"

She tried to act like she didn't know who I was talking to so I yelled again, "Heyyyy, what's your name?"

After she told me her name, I told her to come here, just like that, "Come here girl!!!"

Twenty-three years later, we're still together and I can truly say that meeting my wife was a turning point for me and that's when I started taking my walk with God more seriously. Me and Trina had started going to church on a regular at Tabernacle of Deliverance Full Gospel. It was a Pentecostal church, which I was used to because I was brought up in that faith. Even with all of the fun and freedom I had and trying to reclaim and catch up on everything I had missed while locked up, I kept feeling a pulling on my heart and felt convicted. I knew God was calling me and like the Bible says, when we submit to God, He gives us the power to resist the devil (James 4:7). When it was time, I knew I had to go cold turkey, which meant breaking away from my boys. I had to stop doing some stuff that I had gotten used to and enjoyed doing.

God had given me a new family. The way God operates is so smooth because He empowers you to resist temptation, so that those worldly desires end up going away. But they don't go away immediately. When He sees that you wanna' do right, that's when he sends the Holy Spirit to enable you to do what's right. Truth begets more truth and I realized I had to go cold turkey, from the music I listened to, to the words I used, and even how I spoke. I mean, I submitted to God with *everything* I loved. I had to because my walk with God was just that serious. I am a witness that God will empower you in anything you do in your pursuit to draw closer to Him. And the more you get to know Him and spend time with him, it just becomes easier and easier. And I'm just so grateful for my boys because they understood and supported me and my decision, which is why I respect them so much to this day.

So up until me and Trina got together, my son, Keith Junior had pretty much stayed with my mama for the whole time while I was locked up. I got to see him from time to time when they came to visit but when I got out, one of the first things I had my mind set on was re-connecting with him. He came to stay with me, but when me and Trina moved in together, Keith's mom, Quintina, took him away and I didn't see him again until he was 16. Quintina and I didn't have the best relationship; probably

PK Williams, right, Trina Williams, and grandchildren.

because of the way we got together. We had the typical high school relationship and while I don't remember all the details on how we hooked up, I *do* remember us both being extremely inexperienced. Using protection was always an afterthought anytime we got together until she got pregnant. I remember being terrified to tell my mama because I had so much respect for her. I didn't want to disappoint her with all she had on her plate, so I waited until Quintana was 9 months pregnant. What blew me away was the fact that Mama had a totally different reaction when I told her. She was happy. This was her first grandchild, so she was excited and more than happy to keep him with her, until I got out. When Trina and I got together we kept him until his mom came back and got him, which we weren't expecting. Losing him, after waiting so long to have him in my life, was very hurtful.

So when Trina and I decided to move in together, I was responsible for not only raising my own son, but I also had the responsibility of raising her two kids, who I have always considered my own from day one. About six months after moving in and becoming an "unofficial family," I made it official. I popped the question to Trina with a $99 ring from Kay Jewelers and she stuck around anyway, praise God. Two years later, we got pregnant with the twins, Patrisia and Patrick. I wanted a girl and Trina wanted a boy and God blessed us with both. Fatherhood has truly been such a blessing, although I admit that I was overwhelmed in the beginning. I was

PK and Trina Williams (center) and their children. From the left: Patrick Williams Jr, Marshel Anderson, Patricia Williams, and Terry Anderson (Keith Williams not shown).

so young when Keith was born and had no idea what it meant to be a father, much less how I would take care of a kid. I remember being terrified, but thank God for Mama who stepped in and stood in the gap when I could not. I wasn't in the room when Keith was born, but I was with the twins. It made me thankful and proud that God had given me this second chance at fatherhood and I knew I was going to be present in their lives and really be there for them. The funny thing about fatherhood and marriage is that it matures you to have people depending on you. It makes you want to be a better man and I knew in my heart that I was determined to make it work. I wasn't going to do anything stupid this time around to mess up the life that God allowed me to build for my wife and kids.

Looking back now, we had some really hard times but even during the hard times, I made it work, with God's help. God always makes a way. I remember one particular time when we were short on money and food. I had all these kids looking at me to feed them. So, what did I do? I looked in the ice box and found some ground meat, some spaghetti and some spaghetti sauce. I whipped that stuff up so fast and made a meal that everybody was grateful for. As a man, you always want to be the provider of your household. I grew up lacking so much that I wanted to make sure our kids had everything I didn't have. I wanted to give them all the direction and support and encouragement I didn't have. And honestly, I didn't want my kids to ever think that they had to steal to get what they wanted, like I did.

All things considered, I think we've done a pretty good job raising our kids. With my oldest Keith being in and out of my life so much, I feel like I missed out on a lot with him. Even though he stayed with us for a few years and had the opportunity to be raised with Terry and Marshel, he had a different upbringing from the rest of my kids because of the back and forth. More importantly, he was gone during the time that I feel I could've had the greatest influence in his life. After Quintina came and got him, I didn't see him again until he was 16. She had gotten married to a military guy and they moved around a lot, so we lost touch. I searched high and low, even reached out to her sisters who didn't know where she was. I remember Mama being heartbroken when we couldn't find him, and I was hurt too because I felt it was necessary for him to be with me and that he needed his father in his life. I'll never forget when we were finally reunited.

His Mom and I had agreed that he would come and stay with me again so I went to pick him up and the Negro took off running! I was so hurt and mad, at the same time. I took his bag out of my car and put it back in the house then told his mom I was out!

In my mind, I was thinking I didn't have to put up with this. I had four kids back at home that loved me, so I got in my car and left. It took some time for the wounds to heal but eventually we reunited and have a good relationship now. I'm so proud of him. He is 29, married and retired from the Navy, where he served for six years.

I'm equally proud of Terry, who's 28, and Marshel, who's 26. Even though I got to the party late in their lives, I am thankful that I had the opportunity to impact their lives early. I did the things that I thought a father should do; like getting up, going to work, kissing them and telling them that I loved them, every day. I can't take credit because I never had an example of what a father should be like. The Holy Spirit had to come in and teach me to be something that I didn't know how to be. I remember one of my kid's friends telling me, "Man, Mr. Williams, you sure do get a lot of love around here."

I told him, "That's because I give it."

To me, going to all of their school events, practices, cheerleading camps, etc., has made a difference because it means that we are there and present, plus we have been blessed to have a really good support system. And although Terry had a baby in his senior year, he didn't let that stop him from pursuing his dreams and neither have we.

Me and Trina worked hard to make ends meet so he could go off to college. We stood in the gap just like my mama did for me and took care of the baby, our grandbaby Jacyran, so Terry could pursue a higher education, which is something neither of us has. Even though it turned out that he wasn't a good fit for college, because college is not for everyone, he is on track and has given us another grandbaby named Trey. Our oldest daughter, Marshel, has done well with her life, too, and we are so proud of her. She is one of the youngest supervisors at her job and is in school getting her Business degree. She gave us our precious grandbaby Trinity, which was unexpected; but once again, we rolled with the punches and made sure she had all the support she needed. We like to think of her as the peacemaker and the glue that holds the kids together because they listen to her, sometimes more than they do us.

Our twin boy Pat Pat received an academic scholarship to a school in Brownwood (TX). He didn't like it his first semester, so we brought him back home and now he's selling cars like me, which makes me proud. He's done well for himself and gave us our fourth grandbaby Naveah. Our other twin, Patrisia is the spoiled one. Early on we thought she was going to be a tomboy because she wasn't girly like Marshel. We are proud of her too. She's getting her degree in Kinesiology, Business and Health Studies. Trina has already told her that, "She *betta' not* even think about having a baby no time soon."

Chapter 5

The Apology

Take heed to yourselves; if thy brother sin, rebuke him; and if he repent, forgive him.
~Luke 17:3~

All things considered, I am grateful for my journey and have no regrets. I truly thank God that he let me experience jail at an early age because at that age, I didn't have anything to lose but had a lot to learn. Jail helped me because it gave me an appreciation for life. If I were to go later in life, I believe I would've lost everything.

PK Williams, redeemed.

I will admit that I have been tempted to fall back into my old habit in some ways. In a lot of ways I feel like a cat that has nine lives because God has spared me so many times; from my first thoughts of suicide, to the guy who almost shot me right before the trial, to my cancer scare while I was in prison.

Even in fatherhood, God has spared my life like the time my daughter Marshel was a sophomore in high school and had run off with a guy. Me and her Dad were dead-set on whipping' up on this dude and taking our baby back home one way or another. I remember being in the car on the way to where me and her Dad thought she was, and God clearly saying to me, *"What are you doing son? Man, I got this."* Before I knew it, I had turned around and was back at home. A few days later, she called one of the sisters at the church, Sister Donna, and said she wanted to come home. So, once again, God delivered me and brought our baby back to us.

I know my mama was right when she proclaimed it early on that basically if I didn't do right; things were not going to end well for me. I now know without a doubt that if I hadn't gone to prison, I'd be dead. Prison truly helped me, but not in the way that most people think. Prison doesn't reform you. I came out not-so-much bitter, but just knowing that I wasn't going back because I was not going to mess up again. I said to myself and even told the cats in jail, "I ain't never coming back to be with you rusty Negros!"

I'm going to work, I'm not going to rob anymore and even if I have to work a job making $3 an hour, I'm not coming back! To me, the very people who say the system is created to rehabilitate you have the mindset that you'll be back. Prison really gave me some time to get my thoughts together and figure out what I wanted to do. What do I think my life would've been if I hit the rewind button and just kept my thoughts to myself about "coming up" and never robbed? Well, I'm pretty sure that I wouldn't have gone to college because it wasn't for me. I was a decent enough football player and had some scholarships to smaller schools on the table, but I knew I wasn't on the level to where I would've been a starter. I was avoiding scouts left and right because I just didn't know what I wanted to do.

My brother and my Uncle Ce were there for me as the male figures in my life although I really didn't have anybody just pushing me or guiding me in my decisions. I had a lot of family but never had that support system where somebody just sat me down and asked me what my plans were. So, college for me was the Texas Department of Criminal Justice, the TDJC.

Had I not gone to jail I more than likely would've gotten on permanently at UPS since I went to work there. I never minded working so I probably would've made a decent living and career at UPS, but I know I am where I am supposed to be at this point in my life. After working for Sweetheart for about five years after getting out of prison, I got on with a container company and stayed there for a year before trying my hand at car sales. People had always said I would make a good car salesman because I could "sell ice to an Eskimo," and also because I had the personality for it. A friend of a friend referred me and put in a good word at the dealership. I've been in the business and doing well at it for the last 19 years.

When the movie *Carter High* came out, I was excited and nervous all at the same time because I just wanted our story to be told right and not paint us as thugs like the movie *Friday Night Lights* did. That just wasn't us.

Because Arthur Muhammad, who we call A.J., directed the film and was around when all of it happened. So he had the benefit of knowing all the details and he got it right too. The ESPN *30 for 30* documentary was right on point too. I really liked the fact that it showed the good, the bad and the ugly. It was cool for me to see all that went on behind the scenes, the people we affected, and how they all really felt. I remember there was a scene in the film where Dale Hansen said he thought the media and the community played a part in our bad decision because they glamorized football so much and put us up on a pedestal. I don't put the responsibility on anyone but myself for the part I played in it all. We had people, good people like Coach James and others, giving us good guidance but we just did what we wanted to do and paid the consequences for our actions.

It's really hard for people who know me now to associate me with that person I used to be. They can hardly believe that I did what I did. It really doesn't bother me that people associate me with the scandal anymore because I feel that I am *so* much greater than my past through Christ Jesus. I know who I am as an individual and more importantly, who I am in Christ. I feel that the life that I'm living now speaks for itself. What does bother me and causes me unrest sometimes is when folks associate the robberies with the accomplishments of the team and that what I did tarnished the team, the community and my family because none of them deserve that. I am man and more importantly a child of God; I want to always own up to what I do. That's one of the reasons I had to write this book, as a way to formally apologize to the following people:

The Apology

To my Family: My biggest regret was letting you, my family down and hurting you the way I did; my brother and especially my mama and grandmamma, who both have gone on to glory. And even though Mama always told me that she loved me and wasn't ashamed of me, I know the whole thing brought shame to our family's name and that I was raised better than that. We were a small family, but I knew I was always loved so I could never say that I lacked love in any way. I would be nothing without your love and support through it all.

To the Carter High Coaching Staff: To Coach James, who I admire so much, as well as the other coaches, who taught us how to win on and off the field, how to be young men, and to never give up; which we never did. You all poured into us and gave us everything we needed to be successful. You believed in us and paved the way for us to have great futures and go to college. I now know that all the cussin' outs and the hours spent on the field were out of love because you cared for us like we were your own. It was our own decision that led us to where we ended up and I am so sorry that I let you down.

To my Carter High teammates and classmates: I apologize for all of the shame that you had to endure when you played no part in the wrong I did. I am sorry for the disrespect and ridicule you had to endure when people heard where you were from. Many of you were trying to focus on finishing up, going to college and becoming successful in life but had to put up with a lot of mess because of something we did. Years after and even until this day you guys probably still get scrutiny and may get it for years to come. For that, I apologize too.

From A Letterman to A Better Man

To the Carter High Community (the parents, students, the churches, the community leaders): When the grading controversy was going on, the school district wanted us out of the championship. We not only represented Carter but every other school in the area including Skyline and Kimball. I know you trusted us and believed in us as a football team. You supported us through thick and thin, through the grading controversy and the trial, and we let you down. I know there is nothing I can do to change it, but I just have to thank you again and humbly ask for forgiveness.

I'm often asked what I learned from the whole experience and what I would do differently. Among the many things I would say, especially to the young folks are:

Appreciate Your Freedom: When you go to prison, you are pretty much told what to do when to do, when to do it and in some cases how long you can do it. You have no choice but to eat what is served for breakfast, lunch and dinner at the same time every day and you only have so much time to eat. Everything is about time, even the time you are doing. You have no place to go and even on the prettiest of days, you can't enjoy a run or a walk in the park. On the coldest day, you can't sit by the fireplace and have that cup of coffee with hazelnut cream or even a cup of hot chocolate with marshmallows on the top – two of my favorite things. I appreciate being free and being able to come and go as I please. Even the little things I took for granted, like waking up in my own bed at my own house is priceless. Just to be free is awesome. It hurt me the most not to be with my family.

The Apology

I missed out on the turkey and cornbread dressing that my Mama prepared during the holidays and missing my grandmamma's services was especially rough.

Actions Have Consequences: Please know the law is for the lawless. No matter who you are, you are not above the law. There are consequences to your actions and if you rob people and get caught, you have to face the consequences. Please know also that your actions affect other people who are connected to your family. As a young Black man, we do not have the luxury of making mistakes and hope that we will get a second chance in life. The system is just not set up that way. The system is set up to help and protect our people who are not of color. In the words of W.E.B. DuBois, "A system cannot fail those it was never meant to protect." It's so important to do what is right the first time around.

Learn From Your Experiences: Experiences are truly what you make of them, and although I consider prison to be modern-day slavery, I do understand that right is right and wrong is wrong. To see that a majority of the prison population is either Black or Hispanic makes me know that something is wrong with the system. But again, I made up my mind that I was never going back. And I'm proud to say that none of us who were convicted went back, and that is once again, because we all came from "good stock."

Acknowledgments

Latrina Williams, you are an excellent wife and I am a blessed man to have you. Baby, we've come such a long way in the time we've been together. When I look at so-called power couples, I can say that we are among them with all we've accomplished in our lives and how we've helped shape our kids' and grandkids' lives too. Time has truly taught me that it's not about the ring, money and the houses, but it's about a man and woman coming together and putting God first. I've learned so much from you and I love that crazy bug you have (smiling). Thank you for trusting and believing in me – even when I didn't have anything (*I was fine though*) and for helping to make me a better man. I love you and look forward to us growing old together...

To **Angie Ransome-Jones**, "my book wife," my sister, my friend, my writer. It has been a God-sent pleasure getting to know you and being able to share my story with someone who took complete interest in me. I remember our first meeting and you interviewing me to see if you wanted to do my story. I truly believe that everything was ordered by God because you also are a believer in Jesus Christ. You are so full of energy and always positive about everything; and you can eat, which I love! I won't miss our 6 am calls. You made it easy to tell you who I am and to talk about my family, which I prize. Thank you for taking on my story and now the world will know my testimony because of you. Thank you.

I want to thank my brother **Michael "Mike" Williams**, the only sibling that I have. You exemplify what it means to be a big brother because you took care of me and looked after me like a big brother is supposed to. I love you bro.

Terry Anderson, Marshel Anderson, Patrick Williams, Jr, Patrisia Williams and Keith Williams, I am so grateful that God trusted me with you all. I thank you all for the opportunity to be a Father to you. I did not know what I was doing but I did know that I was going to be there with y 'all no matter what. I hope I have served as an example that a Black man could overcome his past and be a successful husband, father and productive in the community. I love you all and am so proud of you!

To my grandkids, **Jacquran Anderson, Trey Anderson, Trinity McCloud and Nevaeh Williams**, I love you all more than words can express, and I am leaving this legacy to you out of that love. You're too young now, but I hope when you get older I will have made you proud as a Grandad. I love you babies!

To my cousin **Marci Foulton**. I thank God that my Mom and your Mom (my auntie) were so close because it made us close. You look so much like Mama. You were always tough because we treated you like a boy. I love you and will never forget our shenanigans at the 7-11 on Camp Wisdom every morning on the way to school.

To **Pastor Mary Van Zandt**, a woman of strength, a Mother in Zion, a holy woman and a preaching machine! You have always been so full of wisdom and compassion and the fact that you make the best fried apple pies on this side of glory, makes me love you even more. You poured into me and trusted me with the young people when I started off as a Youth Minister and trusted me enough to make me Youth Pastor and I will always love and cherish you for that.

To **Pastor Patrick Giles** – man, when I decided to get back in church, you were (and still are) someone I looked up to. I have always admired how you conduct yourself and remember saying to myself if he's young and can live for God, then I can too! Your life and the way you live it has been a constant source of encouragement for me.

To **Derrick Richardson** (Swift Witness) – my team mate, classmate and brother in the Lord. I have learned so much from you! You are truly a prophet and a man of God. I love the time we spend together just talking on the phone about God and hearing about your experiences with the Lord in your dreams and visions. Class of 1989 CC Baby!!! Love you man.

To my **Auntie Shirley Reynolds** – I knew I was always your baby because you raised me and treated me like I was your own. You are the auntie that was always near and dear to me. I remember even when you and Mama had your disagreements I was always welcome in your home, because that's the type of heart you have. Thank you for taking me in during my senior year and for being the best aunt a man could ever ask for. I love you! Love you!!

Thank you, Uncle **Ce Reynolds** for stepping in, holding our family down and together. You have been such a great role model, mentor, and the father-figure I never had. You brought stability to our family and you showed us how we could be successful in life despite our circumstances.

Knowing that I can always call on you for anything gives me such comfort. You have always made me a priority in your busy life and I cannot thank you enough for always being there for me.

To my **Auntie Renetta Williams**, thank you for always loving all of Unc's nieces and nephews as if we were your own and for keeping him (and us) well fed. I love you and your greens more than words can say!

To **Pastor Victor Lee** – Man, I have learned so much from you on how to be transparent and to stand in my truth. You have shown me how to have fun and still be saved! The way you love God and you your wife and family has taught me how to love God first and my wife and family second. You have also shown me how to love people, regardless of how they act, because they are God's people. Thank you for being such a great example to me and to the congregation. I love how we can just sit down and break bread together and openly talk about anything. I love you Pastor Lee.

To the late, great **Rosie Austin** of Lighthouse Church of God In Christ, you spoke this book into my life in the late 90's and now it has come to pass. Even though you have gone on to be with the Lord, I have to thank you for sowing into my life. I'll never forget that when I came before the Church and asked for forgiveness, you and many of the other mothers came and hugged me and prayed for me and spoke life and forgiveness into me. I remember you coming to pick me up bringing me to prayer when I didn't have a way. I never experienced God's love in the way I experienced it with you. It was an honor and a privilege to have known you.

Acknowledgments

To **Mother Dora Bell and Family (Joe Jr, Doug, James & Donna Grant)** - you all have served as a backbone for me and my family in that you've been with us through the good and the bad. Thank you for all the memories. Although Mother Bell is gone, I'll never forget her strength, the spiritual connection she had with God and the way she taught us how to pray and stand up against the enemy! Many times, she spoke life into me and my family, and every word she spoke has come to pass. I remember preaching on many occasions and her coming to church sick as a dog. She would just lay on the front pew because she simply wanted to be in God's presence and surrounded by God's people. Even though I miss her, I am glad she is resting with the Lord now. My love to you all.

To **Jessie Armstead**, my former teammate and an all-around cool dude – I just want to thank you for making a good decision to not get involved with what we were doing. You turned out to be someone that we came to look up to. I'm glad you didn't get involved – turned out to be a five-time pro-bowler a former New York Giant, and now a prominent businessman.

Special thanks to **Nadirah Hill**, who served as Angie's research assistant in the writing process. As my age increases, my memory does the opposite, so I appreciate you keeping me (and Angie) honest with your research and fact-checking skills. Best of wishes in your studies at UNT!

To **Lisa Renee Johnson, Marissa Monteilh and Ms. Lisa Bell**: Although I have yet to meet you both, I understand you were both the inspiration behind Angie agreeing to write my story. You helped guide her through the process and she did an excellent job, so you both have blessed me through your influence! Thank you!

To my **Chacon Autos family, Chris Chaney, Gary Chaney, Darrell Chaney:** Thank you all for the opportunity to work for such a great company! I never imagined that I could make the money that I've been blessed to make. This allowed me to take care of my family, which I appreciate. I remember when I had my second home built and you all showed up because you were so happy to see your employees prosper. Thank you for giving me the opportunity to work for such a great company.

Special thanks to the **family of the late Elder Calloway and my church family at the Light House Church of God In Christ (Dallas, TX)**, which is my spiritual birthing place. John 3:5-6 says it all….

To the **family of the late Pastor Van Zandt, Pastor Mary Van Zandt, and my church family at the Tabernacle of Deliverance (Dallas, TX)** – You have served as my foundation. I learned so many things from you all, which has prepared me for my "now." Thank you, Pastor for the rebuke you gave me, because it was done out of love. Learning how to be a servant, how to seek God and how to fast and pray, were all essential to my growth. I've seen miracles performed and prophecies come to pass at the Tabernacle of Deliverance, which have all been life-altering experiences to me. You all taught me that Jesus is King!!! I thank for that and appreciate the love you showed my mama when she came to serve. You took her in and loved her and when she went home to be with the Lord, you all were there. Your church will

Acknowledgments

always be my church home and your Pastor will always be my Pastor.

To **Pastor Victor Lee and First Lady Keatre Lee, my battle buddy, and the rest of my family at Chosen Church (Dallas, TX).** – Because of the foundation you have provided, I have been able to pour into others through my preaching of the Word. I know that at times, I can be long-winded, so I appreciate your patience with me as I try to work on that. Thank you for loving me and accepting me as your Assistant Pastor, and for the support you have shown me and my family since my arrival. I love you all.

To my boys **Keith Campbell, Carlos Allen and Derrick Evans** – Like I've always said, we came from good stock, so we did not allow our mistakes to define us. Instead, we learned and have grown from them. Ecclesiastes 7: 8-14 says, "Better is the end of a thing than the beginning thereof." Now that we are able to give back to our families and community, we are better and successful Black Men! I love you my brothers.

Pastor Sultan Cole, my childhood friend, we grew up playing Star Wars and we even spent several holidays together. My mama and your mama were the best of friends. Thank you for allowing me to preach to your congregation on several times, and I do understand I went over but you were ok with that. I truly respect you. Love you my brother.

To **Beverly Johnson**, my spiritual sister – You always know how to make me laugh and to say the right things at the right time. Thank you for being an ear for me and my wife and always pointing us in the right direction. We grew up together in ministry and you have seen me grow into a man. I love you **Lonnie Johnson, Ashley Johnson and Rethia Johnson**.

To my "other brother," **Vincent Burell**, the only other man I trust with my wife (smile). You have been there for me and my family, both financially and emotionally. Thank you for always being a listening ear. I love you brother and thank you for just being you.

To **Don Goodacre, Rickey Brown and Gabe Tolden**, thank you for being in my inner circle and I really appreciate you all. Thank you all for always being a confidential "sounding board" that I can trust. I love you three, you are my "dawgs!"

Bishop Porter Perry, I want to thank you for taking time out of your busy schedule to counsel us on several occasions, without judgement or bias. I admire you for being such a soft-spoken, but powerful man. The anointing is definitely on your life. I love you and the entire **Perry family**.

To "my little sister," **Ladondra Wilson** – I am so proud of the woman you have become. Thank you for believing in me and pushing me to this point. And thank you for the connection with Angie. This project could not have come to fruition without you. I love you Don Don!

To "my team," **Derrick Walker, Shelia Brown, Tish Jones and Vickie Savage** – Thank you all so much for believing in me. We are family now, CC4LIFE! Love you guys.